doubt!!

DOUBT

Chapter 5

BE STRAIGHT WITH ME, AI-AI... YOU'RE A SEX MACHINE, AREN'T YOU?
NO, I'M NOT.

YES, YOU ARE! YOU ARE TOTALLY A SECRET NYMPHO.
Naughty!
GRRR

WOULD YOU JUST DROP IT?!
I BET YOU'VE DONE IT WAY MORE THAN ME...

Chiharu Hamano

Of all the characters in DOUBT!! she's the easiest one to draw. Therefore you should expect to see her often!

I live in a wonder-land...

FINALS SCHEDULE

MODERN JAPANESE	POLITICS	ENGINEERING	CHEMISTRY
ENGLISH (GRAMMAR)	BIOLOGY	ENGLISH (READING)	CLASSIC JAPANESE
ALGEBRA		GEOMETRY	

FINALS START TOMORROW AND I'M NOT READY! O, WOE! I'M WAVERING ON A PRECIPICE! PEERING INTO AN ABYSS!

YEAH, WELL, I FAILED LAST TIME! I'M ON A FIRST-NAME BASIS WITH THAT ABYSS!

LIKE LAST NIGHT? I TOOK A STUDY BREAK AND BEFORE I KNEW IT I'D BEEN WATCHING THE HOME SHOPPING NETWORK FOR FOUR HOURS!

I MEMORIZED THEIR ENTIRE CATALOG!

Also, that host Jeffrey is cute.

I WIN!

YOU IDIOT.

CONGRAT-ULATIONS, YOU'RE IN THE DEEPEST. YOU MUST BE VERY PROUD.
HA HA
WHY WOULD YOU BRAG ABOUT SOME-THING LIKE THAT?
LAUGH IT UP. YOU'LL DO FINE-- YOU GUYS ARE SMART.
AI-AI, TOO ...
I *WISH*... I'VE BEEN SO BUSY I HAVEN'T HAD TIME TO STUDY. I'M WAY BEHIND. ESPECIALLY IN ENGLISH...
HEE HEE
ENGLISH
STUDENT TEACHER
CHIHARU HAMANO
13HR

SIGH
AI-CHAN, YOU WANNA BORROW MY NOTES?
He takes awesome notes.
NO WAY! I WANNA SEE YOUR NOTES, YU-CHAN!
NOT YOU.
WHY MUST YOU BE SO CRUEL? WE COULD DO WHATEVER YOU WANTED...!
I *WANT* YOU TO LET GO OF ME!
GAHHH!!
CLK
ZZUP
HOW ABOUT YOU? ARE YOU READY?
NAH. I'VE BEEN BAD AT ENGLISH SINCE JUNIOR HIGH.
ENGLISH IS EASY ONCE YOU NAIL THE BASICS!

THANKS, SENSEI. OKAY IF WE COME BACK?
SHE'S TOTALLY EASY TO TALK TO.
Students Prohibited During
MY DOOR IS ALWAYS OPEN ...
SWIVEL
...TO STUPID BRATS WHO ARE TOO DUMB TO BREATHE !!
Eech...
TEACHERS' LOUNGE
OVERWORKED, UNDERPAID... AND I HAVE TO TUTOR THOSE STUPID LITTLE TRAMPS.
They think they're cute because they're young.
I'D MUCH RATHER TUTOR THE BOYS. ESPECI-ALLY...
THAT ONE ...
13 HR

MY PLACE? FOR A STUDY GROUP ...?
YUP. YOU LIVE THE CLOSEST.
B-BUT... IT'S A WRECK ...
SÔ ... ♥
WHO CARES ?! IT'S FINE.
HA! AI-AI, YOU'RE NER-VOUS ...
...NEVER HAD A BOY IN YOUR ROOM BEFORE? I SMELL A VIRGIN!
Y-YOU COULD SMELL... THAT?
Hit a nerve.
THRUST
STROKE
HUH?!

DON'T WORRY... I DON'T SMELL ANY-THING.
SNIFF
...
BLUSH
OKAY, FINE! COME OVER AFTER SCHOOL, OKAY?
Piece of cake.
SMACK
Hustler ...
MAE-KAWA'S PLACE? I WANNA GO.
GIVE IT UP. ICHINOSE BARELY GOT IN. SHE'S BEAUTIFUL AND SHE'S PURE, DUDE.
IT'S NOT LIKE I DON'T **WANT** THEM TO COME OVER...
SHUDDER

HEH ...

WHAT'S WITH THE ICY SMILE ?!

AAAHH!!

TICK

ACK! WHAT A MESS!
THIS IS EXACTLY WHY I DON'T INVITE PEOPLE OVER!!
I GOTTA HIDE ALL THIS STUFF BEFORE SÔ-KUN SHOWS UP...
RUSH
RUSH
HOME: A MINE-FIELD OF HORRORS...
...HUMILIATION BOMBS, SCATTERED HAPHAZARDLY...
ANIME THEME SONG
CUTIE HONEY
HURRICANE OF LOVE
An anime CD?! What was I thinking...?
A PHOTO OF JIMI AI... NOW, THIS IS A SERIOUS LAND MINE...
NYANKO
GAK!
What was up with that T-shirt...?
I KNOW THEY KNOW, BUT IF THEY ACTUALLY SEE... I DON'T THINK SÔ-KUN COULD TAKE IT. BETTER HIDE IT!
Huh...? What's this?

"MY TEARS UNDER SHADOWS OF STARS" BY AI

O! SWEET AND LONELY HEART! HOW THOU DOST SPRINKLE, TEARDROPS THAT TWINKLE, TWINKLE LIKE THE SMALLEST STARS! O! LONELY STARS....

(AN EXCERPT FROM A POEM AI WROTE DURING HER JIMI ERA)

Better hide this!

EEEK!

It's illustrated, too.

HOURS LATER ...

DING DONG

SPARKLE

HELLO!

Out of uniform ...♥
SÔ-CHAN'S ON HIS WAY.
COME ON IN.
Hm...
LET'S WORK IN THE LIVING ROOM, OKAY? MY ROOM IS TINY.
AS LONG AS I DON'T LET THEM IN MY ROOM, IT'LL BE FINE...
Smug
HUH.
Nice.
I'VE BEEN CLEAN-ING LIKE A MANIAC.
I TOOK MOM'S MAGAZINES OUT AND REPLACED THEM WITH COOL ONES.
DING DONG
I LEFT NO STONE UN-TURNED!
ALL THAT'S MISS-ING IS SÔ-KUN ...
Yes!

HELLO THERE!
I RAN INTO HER ON THE WAY AND SHE FOLLOWED ME HERE.
TEACHERS GET OUT EARLY DURING FINALS, TOO.
HUH, NICE HOUSE.
SLAM
HOLD ON ...
THAT BITCH...! DOES SHE THINK SHE CAN WORM IN ON MY CHANCE TO SPEND TIME WITH SÔ-KUN-- WHEN I'M RISKING HAVING HIM IN MY HOUSE?!
THANKS FOR HAVING ME...
OH WOW, IT'S REALLY NICE. ♡
SLIP SLIP

⇨ Closed the door behind her (like a salesman).

THIS REMINDS ME OF WHEN I USED TO GIVE YOU PRIVATE LESSONS, SÔ.
"SHE DID STUFF JUST LIKE THIS WHEN SHE WAS DATING SÔ."
WHAT'S THAT SUPPOSED TO MEAN ?!
NO FAIR! I WISH I'D KNOWN SÔ-KUN IN JUNIOR HIGH...
Hee Hee ...
HOW DID SHE WEASEL HER WAY INTO MY HOUSE...?!
HEY, WHO'S AT THE DOOR? SÔ-CHAN?
Even if she is his ex...

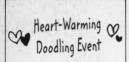

Izumi's Family Portrait

Part 1

◀ Izumi's Mother ▶

Power Points:	5000
Forgetfulness:	∞
	(beyond measure)

She lectures me every time I go home:

You're gonna kill yourself! You're working yourself to death! You'll die!

That's her prophecy, I guess. True, my health has suffered since I started doing manga, but... does she really think she's helping...?

She followed me.

SÔ-CHAN! WHAT'S THE STORY?!

HEH. WHY, I'M HERE AS YOUR PRIVATE TUTOR! ♡

GAH! WHAT IS THAT WOMAN DOING HERE?!

...IT'S LIKE, THANKS BUT NO THANKS, YOU KNOW?

Yuichiro-kun!

Yes!

I DON'T THINK IT'S A GOOD IDEA FOR YOU TO HANG OUT WITH US RIGHT BEFORE FINALS ...
I DON'T WANT THE SCHOOL TO FIND OUT AND ACCUSE US OF CHEAT-ING.
YEAH, RIGHT.
WE BOTH KNOW CHIHARU'S NOT GONNA LEAVE UNLESS I DO.
PAT
DON'T LET THE DOOR HIT YOU ON THE...
...
C'MON, NOW ...
WE DO NEED A TUTOR. AND AS LONG AS NOBODY FINDS OUT, WE'LL BE FINE, RIGHT?
Sô-kun has to stay...
Yeah... okay.
GOOD.
NOW IF THIS GETS OUT, AT LEAST WE'LL ALL FAIL TOGE-THER!

SÔ!!
HA HA! DID I SAY THAT OUT LOUD ...?
I'M HUNGRY...
LETHARGIC
HUP
LET'S HAVE SOME OF THE CAKE I BROUGHT.
MAY I USE YOUR KITCHEN?
OH, I'LL GET IT!
SHE'S TRYING TO SHOW OFF!!

NOT SO FAST, CHIHA-RU!!
FAUOHON TEA APPLE TEA
BAM
HEH...
I'LL FIX US SOME TEA.
WHSHH...
TAP WATER? NOT BOTTLED ?!
SHOVE SHOVE
TAP WATER IS OXY-GENATED AND IT TASTES BETTER!
CRACK
CRACK
WAIT! CALM DOWN ...!
WHAT WOULD THAT KYOKO KANO* DO IN THIS SITUATION? THINK...

*Kyoko Kano, a famous TV personality in Japan, is an outspoken feminist with a va-va-voom hourglass figure. Earlier, Ai's classmates at her new school compared her to K.K.

SPARKLE
LOOK AT US QUARRELING OVER SOMETHING SO MINOR! IT'S JUST SILLY.
→ Through gritted teeth!
YOU'RE ABSOLUTELY RIGHT. AFTER ALL, WITH A CHEAP TEA LIKE THAT, BOTTLED WATER WOULDN'T MAKE MUCH DIFFERENCE, WOULD IT? ♡
Tee Hee...
GAH!
SHE'S REALLY GOOD! YEARS OF PRACTICE, I GUESS...
POP
HEY, IS IT OKAY IF I MAKE COFFEE?
SÔ!
L-LET ME ...!
GLUG
GLUG

CRAAAASH
OW...
HOT...
I-I'M SORRY! YOU'RE GETTING BURNED!! QUICK... OFF! OFF!
RATTLE
WHAT WAS THAT NOISE ...?

WHOA!
A THREE-WAY IN THE *KITCHEN*?! WHAT ARE YOU RUNNING HERE, A BROTHEL?
WAIT-- NO! I CAN EXPLAIN!
MORE LIKE A ZOO.
My trunks are stained.
IT'S OKAY, ELEPHANT-SAN.
Hoom-pra!
EEEK!

PUT THAT AWAY!!
I saw it. I saw it. I saw it!
They're wet.
AI-CHAN! THIS IDIOT NEEDS A CHANGE OF--
I'LL FIND HIM SOMETHING!
I'LL GET IT!
She's still trying to prove something.
DASH DASH DASH
What the...?
CLATCH
HM?
OH...
THIS MUST BE AI-AI'S ROOM.
THAT'S OKAY. HER SWEAT-PANTS SHOULD FIT HIM.

CREAK
WHAT'S THIS STUFF IN HERE FOR...?
WAIT JUST A SEC !!
YOU DON'T NEED TO RAN-SACK MY ENTIRE ROOM !!
SLAM
WHAT?! I WASN'T --
YOU'RE HIDING SOME-THING, AREN'T YOU?
NO! I JUST DON'T NEED YOU POKING AROUND --

ULP!
LOOK AT HER EYES!! SHE KNOWS!
CREAK
HEY! I FOUND AI-AI'S YEARBOOK!
WHAT'S IN THIS ENVELOPE ...?
AI-AI, WHICH OF THESE IS YOU?
HEY! DON'T TOUCH THAT--!
DASH DASH DASH DASH
WHOOSH
GIVE IT BACK! THAT'S NOT YOURS!

SLAM
WHAT WAS THAT?
NO CLUE.
UM, HEY...
AI-AI JUST CHASED CHIHARU OUT OF THE HOUSE.
HONK
HONK
Huff
UGH... WHAT WAS I THINKING...
Huff
...LETTING HER INTO THAT MINEFIELD...?
WHERE DID YOU GO, CHIHARU?!

BOO!!

PRETTY HIGH UP, HUH? ♡

!!

COULDN'T JUST WALK AWAY FROM A FALL LIKE THAT, COULD YOU...?

HONK HONK

I'LL LET YOU GO THIS TIME, BUT...
...KEEP HANGING AROUND SÔ, AND NEXT TIME YOU WON'T BE SO LUCKY.
HUFF
HUFF
SO WHAT IS THIS STUFF, ANY-WAY ...?
"'MY TEARS UNDER SHADOWS OF STARS' BY AI. O! SWEET AND LONELY HEART!"
NOOO!
DO YOU HAVE TO READ IT *OUT LOUD* ?!
YOU THINK YOU'RE SOMETHING SPECIAL BECAUSE YOU TURNED YOURSELF AROUND, DON'T YOU? WELL, YOU'RE NOT SPECIAL...
YOU'RE A FAKE. A FRAUD. SO UN-SURE, I SHOULD CALL YOU 'MISS DOUBT'...
FLUSH
Campus
BUH-BYE.
STUMBLE

TRIP

ACK!

FLID

UH OH. LOOKS LIKE YOU'RE IN BIG TROUBLE ...

JOLT

GRAB

Heh...

IF YOU THINK I'M GONNA SAVE YOU, SWEETIE, YOU'RE MISTAKEN. ♡

HEY! STOP THAT!

PULL...

NOOO! I'LL FALL! LET GO OF ME!
LET GO!
...YOU'RE THE ONE WHO'S MIS-TAKEN, SWEETIE.
WHAT IS YOUR PROBLEM, HUH? YOU DON'T EVEN KNOW!
DO YOU KNOW WHAT IT'S LIKE TO BE SO PLAIN THAT BOYS DON'T EVEN KNOW YOUR NAME?
CAN YOU IMAGINE HOW I FELT WHEN HE NOTICED ME? WHEN HE SAID ...
"AI-CHAN!"
LET GO!
LET ME GO!!

YOU'RE MORE THAN WILLING TO KICK ME DOWN...
...HOW DARE YOU BE SUR-PRISED WHEN I KICK BACK?!

...EEK.

THAT'S ENOUGH, AI-CHAN ...

C'MON ...
THIS IS A BAD SPOT FOR A STREET FIGHT.
YOU'RE PRETTY FAST! I HAD A HARD TIME FINDING YOU...
HOIST
W-WAH ...

WAHHH!!
IT'S OKAY.
SÔ ...
CHIHA-RU...
I HAD SOME GOOD TIMES WITH YOU...
I LIKED BEING HELD IN THOSE SOFT ARMS.
BUT THINGS ARE DIFFERENT NOW, AND I COULD SNAP THOSE ARMS IN HALF IF I HAD TO.
I'M NOT SAYING I *WILL*, I'M SAYING I *COULD*.
YOU UNDER-STAND ?

LET'S GO, AI-CHAN.
HONK HONK HONK
...
WHAT'S WRONG?
IT'S JUST THAT I...
...I LOVE YOU SO MUCH ...

ONE WEEK LATER ...
13HR
THE TIME HAS COME FOR GOOD-BYES, SO I JUST WANT TO SAY THAT I HAVE ENJOYED BEING YOUR STUDENT TEACHER...
THERE WERE TIMES WHEN I COULDN'T KEEP UP WITH YOU, I KNOW...
BUT ...
FARE-WELL, MY ARCH-ENEMY!
It's all behind us now...
I'LL WORK HARD, AND SOON I'LL BE BACK ...
NOT AS A STUDENT, BUT AS A FULL-TIME TEACHER !!

THE TYPHOON SEASON PASSED, AND THE HEIGHT OF SUMMER WAS APPROACHING ...
YECCH!!
SWELTER
SWELTER
...BUT CHIHARU WAS NOT FORGOT-TEN.
I FAILED ENGLISH ?!
WHOA, YUICHIRO! YOU HAVE A COLD?
ACHOO!
YES! BECAUSE YOU STOLE MY PANTS TO CHASE AFTER AI-CHAN!
I also bombed the test, thanks to you.
OH! I STILL HAVE SÔ-KUN'S UNDER-WEAR AT HOME ...

doubt!!

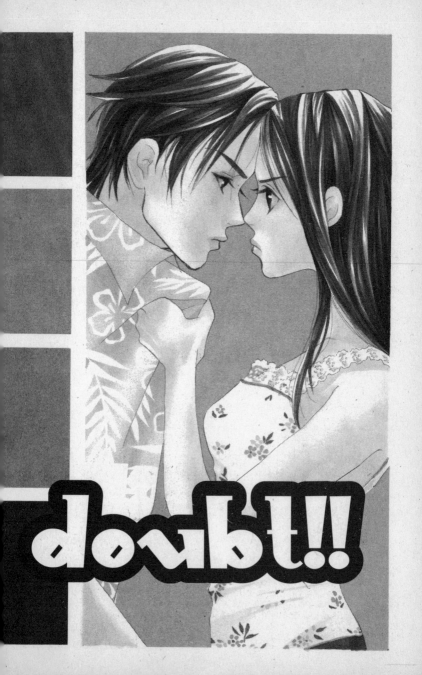

Chapter 6

DOU BT!

SUMMER VACATION!!
MY ONLY GOAL USED TO BE TO FINISH MY SUMMER ASSIGN-MENTS BY THE END OF JULY...
HEH...
Done! Two summers in a row...
SO LONG, SUCKER. I HAVE BEEN REBORN!
AI MAEKAWA, 16 YEARS OLD
FLUTTER
THIS SUMMER, I'M GONNA SHINE!!

SWELTER
SWELTER
I CAN'T FOCUS WHEN IT'S THIS HOT. CAN'T THEY GET US A/C?
HA HA!
YOU SHOULD GO MEDI-TATE ON TREES OR SOME THING... YOU KNOW, COOL OUT.
PAT
PAT
PAT
PAT
ANYWAY, IT'S ALMOST VACA-TION...

Yuichiro Kato

Sometimes, the more normal a person is, the worse things turn out for him. That's just life. I do feel sorry for him, though... a little. Maybe I should let him take a more active role...?

So many unexpected sorrows
...

WHOOSH!

HEY!

SORRY!
PAT
PAT
...
... COOL OUT ?
Right...
YEAH, WELL ...
IT'S HARD TO BELIEVE SHE USED TO BE A NERD...
NO WONDER SHE GOT THAT MAGA- ZINE FEATURE.
WHAT ?
DIDN'T YOU KNOW ?
Sigh...
SHE'S OUT OF MY LEAGUE, THAT'S FOR SURE. PLUS, I HEARD SHE'S DATING ICHI- NOSE...
13HR

WHY'D YOU GET CALLED TO THE OFFICE?
SO THEY COULD REMIND ME I'M A STUDENT AND NOT A CELEBRITY, I GUESS...
SHUT
HMPH. THEY'RE JUST JEALOUS BECAUSE NONE OF THEM ARE IN MAGA-ZINES.
Cool Street
SNATCH
LEMME SEE ...
"SUMMER'S HERE AND THERE'S ONE SPOT WHERE YOU'RE SURE TO GET LUCKY. JUST ASK 18-YEAR-OLD ARISA..." ♡
WRONG PAGE !!
BLUSH

DATA
7
AI MAEKAWA-CHAN
FRESHMAN
"I HOPE TO SPEND THE SUMMER WITH A BOYFRIEND."
NEXT MONTH
"Lose weight for bikini season ..."
Wrong!
YU-CHAN! I'M IN THE MAGAZINE, TOO. CHECK IT OUT!
RATTLE...
HUH. NOT BAD.
REALLY? YOU LIKE IT?
MINA, I DON'T SEE YOU HERE...
LOOK CLOSELY...
...
See?
HEY, AI-CHAN. THERE'S A MIDGET ON YOUR SHOULDER.
AN EVIL SPIRIT, MAYBE? DEFINITELY EVIL, ANYWAY.
Exorcism, anyone?
WHAT DID YOU CALL ME?!

I CAN'T BELIEVE I'M FEATURED IN A MAGAZINE...
TH-THUMP TH-THUMP
HEY, DO YOU KNOW A MAGAZINE CALLED "COOL STREET"?
Mind if we take your picture?
LET'S GET OUT OF HERE, MINA! THEY JUST WANT TO PHOTOGRAPH US FOR SOME NAUGHTY SCHOOLGIRL PICTORIAL...
In a porno mag!
HUH ...?
STRANGERS NEVER USED TO TALK TO ME ON THE STREET UNLESS THEY WANTED TO TRICK ME...
Or sell me something...
SOB...
JEALOUS!
I BET THEY'RE GOING TO CALL YOU IN FOR PHOTO SHOOTS NOW...
THEY ALREADY ASKED ME TO DO ONE OVER SUMMER BREAK, BUT I'M NOT GOING TO...
I'VE GOT MORE IMPORTANT THINGS TO DO.
Plus, the teachers are mad.
WHAAAAT?!
THIS SUMMER I'M DETERMINED TO WIN THE HEART OF SÔ-KUN!!
No mercy!
No mercy!

A CHANCE TO SPEND SOME QUALITY TIME TOGETHER... THE TWO OF US, ALONE...
I TOLD YOU! I DON'T WANT TO DO A PHOTO SHOOT.
I'm helpless!!
YOU CAN'T PASS UP A CHANCE LIKE THIS, AI-AI.
THEY'RE PICKING YOU UP HERE, RIGHT?
LOOK
LOOK
SHE'S MY BAIT... THEY'LL NOTICE ME THIS TIME!
I DON'T HAVE ANYTHING BETTER TO DO.
This might be a laugh...
I'M TOO BROKE TO DO ANY-THING ELSE.
GRIN
GRIN
GRIN
HA HA!
C'MON, WE'RE HERE TO CHEER YOU ON!
NOOOO!!
YOU'RE LATE!!

I'M WITH "COOL STREET"... YOU'RE THE READER MODEL, RIGHT?
YES... OKAY...
TWO GIRLS, TWO BOYS... THAT'S EVERY-ONE. LET'S GO!
WAIT, BUT--!
SHOVE
GET ON THE BUS!
BUT THESE ARE--
WE'RE PRESSED FOR TIME! JUST GET IN!
VROOOOM
THIS IS THE PLACE, RIGHT?
DID THEY LEAVE WITHOUT US? WE'RE NOT *THAT* LATE...

WHAT?!
THEY'RE NOT MODELS ?!
WE'RE ALMOST THERE! WE DON'T HAVE TIME TO TURN AROUND NOW!
I'M SORRY. I TRIED TO TELL YOU, BUT--
HA HA HA!
DON'T BEAT YOURSELF UP, MISTER. EVERYBODY MAKES MISTAKES.
PAT
I'M NOT BEATING MYSELF UP!
WHEW.
Thanks, Sō-kun.
THIS WILL WORK FINE, WON'T IT?
HEH HEH
PEEK

I'M THE STYLIST, AND I SAY THESE KIDS...
...ARE BETTER LOOKING THAN THE REAL MODELS!
OF COURSE THEY ARE! JUST LOOK AT HIM!
... FINE.
SCRATCH SCRATCH
HE HAS AN ATTRACTIVE FACE... HIS PERSONALITY ASIDE.
AND THAT ONE, HE LOOKS LIKE A DOLL. A TRADITIONAL BOY, I SUPPOSE.
Ech!
AND...
Hello! ♡

Folk Art.
A BLACK COW?
THAT WAS LOW! I SHOULD KILL THIS GUY, RIGHT?
GAK!!
FINE, FINE!! WE'LL USE HER! BUT PUT HER BACK IN HER CAGE UNTIL WE'RE READY TO SHOOT!
WOW.

THE OCEAN ...
IT'S PER-FECT!
WOOZY
WOW... IT FINALLY FEELS LIKE SUMMER. AREN'T YOU GLAD YOU CAME?
UM... AI-CHAN ?
CHATTER
YOU DIZZY ?
IS SHE OKAY ?
CHATTER
TH-THAT'S NOT IT.
IT'S JUST THAT IT'S SO PERFECT ...
OCEAN
COOL BOY (FUTURE BOYFRIEND)
MAGAZINE CREW
COM-PARED WITH LAST YEAR...
PUBLIC POOL
PEEING BRAT
NERDY FRIENDS (BOTH SINGLE)
She's crying ...

THIS IS THE BEST SUMMER VACATION EVER!!
SHE SEEMS OKAY.
THAT'S OKAY ...?
OKAY, IF YOU'VE ALL CHANGED, LET'S SHOOT ...
EVERY-BODY SMILE ...
CLICK
YOU LOOK A LITTLE STIFF... RELAX, YOU'RE SUPPOSED TO BE HAV-ING FUN, REMEM-BER? ♡
LET'S TRY IT...
CLICK

Yeah!!
...LIKE THIS!
YOU MEAN, LIKE WE'RE HAVING A SEI-ZURE?
WHAT-EVER. JUST DO IT!!
HA HA HA!
I THINK I'M GETTING AN ULCER... AND WE STILL HAVE TO SHOOT THEM IN SWIMSUITS AND YUKATA!
RELAX. LOOK! FOR THE LOVERS' SCENE ...
...THOSE TWO-- THEY WON'T EVEN HAVE TO ACT.
WHAT ...?

LOVERS...? SHE THINKS WE'RE LOVERS!
WOW...
That's awe-some...
...
AI-CHAN REALLY LIKES SÔ, I GUESS.
TAKE FIVE, EVERY-BODY!
ROLL
MELON SODA
KIRIN
POCARI SWEAT
BODY REQUEST
HM... I WANT PO-CARI.
AFTER-NOON TEA!
THE PO-CARI'S MINE!
...
Left over.
MELON SODA
YUI-CHIRO-KUN ...?

WANT A POCARI?
COOL
FLUTTER
GUYS USUALLY DON'T WANT THE SWEET DRINKS.
Let's trade.
BUT THIS ONE'S--
--WATER-MELON, I KNOW. IT'S FINE... I LIKE IT.
BESIDES, YOU'RE TOO NICE...

YOU WORRY SO MUCH ABOUT OTHERS ...
YOU SHOULD LOOK OUT FOR WHAT *YOU* WANT EVERY NOW AND THEN, RIGHT?
YES! DEMAND WHAT YOU DESIRE! THAT'S HOW I SHOULD APPROACH SÔ-KUN!!
LET'S GO!
KILL ME ...
POP
BATHING SUITS! PRETTY KILLER, RIGHT?

SHUT UP, MO-RON !!
What's your problem ...?
Hmph.
MY PROBLEM IS YOU. YOU TOOK THE BEST DRINK AND THE BEST SWIM TRUNKS-- AND YOU DIDN'T EVEN ASK!
Not that I'm surprised.
WHAT? YOU WANT THIS SUIT?
GAHH!
FINE.
I DON'T WANT IT NOW! IT'S ALREADY BEEN DEFILED WITH THE WARMTH OF YOUR CROTCH!
SCHWOOP
YUI-CHI-RO...
HOIST
!

TRYING TO BE CUTE?
WHAT'S WITH YOU, HUH?
TALK TO ME.
IT'S--
...
LET GO!
JUST CALM DOWN AND LET IT WORK ITSELF OUT... DAMMIT.
SLAP
SIGH...
YOU CAN'T EVEN SPEAK UP FOR YOURSELF, YOU BIG BABY...
WHOOSHHH
SÔ ...
snap

IF THERE WAS A GIRL YOU LIKED, WHAT WOULD YOU DO?
I'D TELL HER.
WHAT IF ANOTHER GUY LIKED HER, TOO?
I'D KICK HIS ASS, IF I HAD TO.
CRUNCH
SKIDDD

WHAT ...?
...I WAS JUST FOLLOWING YOUR ADVICE.
SIGH...
... SCREW YOU.
YOU PUNCHED ME FULL OUT. YOU HAVEN'T DONE THAT SINCE WE WERE KIDS.
GUYS! GUYS! WHAT ARE YOU DOING ?!

CRACK
NO! THE SHOOT! STOP THEM!
DON'T WORRY! I'M KICKING HIS ASS MINEUCHI-STYLE.*
THUD
THERE'S NO MINEUCHI WITH FISTS, YOU IDIOT!
NO...! THE CLOTHES ...!
They're expen-sive...
SHIFT SHIFT
I HAVE TO PAY FOR ANY DAMAGE ...
Ulp!
STOP IT!

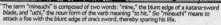

*The term "mineuchi" is composed of two words: "mine," the blunt edge of a katana-sword blade, and "uchi," the noun form of the verb meaning "to hit." So "mineuchi" means to attack a foe with the blunt edge of one's sword, thereby sparing his life.

Whoa...

WHY ...?

HEH ...

HA HA... SORRY, AI-CHAN. I DECIDED TO TAKE YOUR ADVICE, TOO.
SHOVE

Izumi's Family Portrait

Part 2

◀ Izumi's Father ▶

Power Points: 2000
Japanese Businessman Points: 100000

My father is frequently sent overseas on business. He recently returned from a long stay in China, and now... whenever he sees Chinese images on TV...

Hi-yaaah!
Oolong Tea!
SHF SHF

...he starts to practice Tai Chi (something kinda like it, anyway).

I wonder what happened in China.

I can't ask him, though... because I feel sorry for him. Being a company man isn't easy, you know?

I THINK YOU SHOULD DATE ME INSTEAD OF SÔ.
ANY OBJECTIONS?

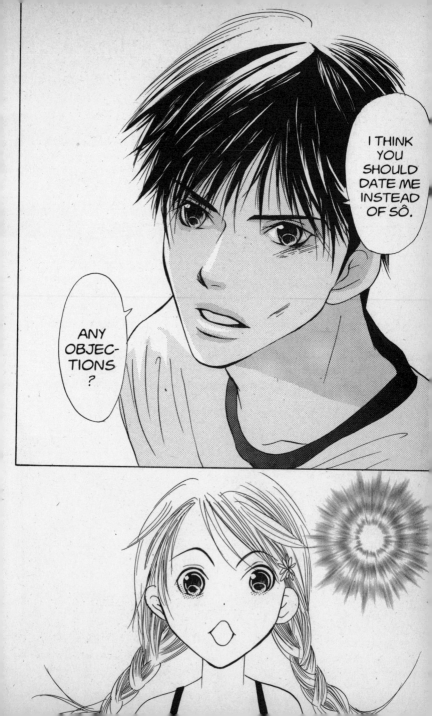

WHOOSHHH
...HEH.
AH HA HA HA!
SCREECH
I'M NOT KIDDING.
ANY OBJECTIONS?
IT'S NOT LIKE I OBJECT, EXACTLY...
GREAT! THEN WE'RE ON?
WH...
...WHAAT?!
AS OF RIGHT NOW, WE'RE A THING.
HE DOESN'T EVEN SEEM LIKE THE SAME GUY!!

DASH
DASH
DA
WAIT ONE COTTON-PICKIN' MINUTE!
SWOOSH
HUFF HUFF
AI-AI, YOU PROMISED! YU-CHAN IS MINE!
I KNOW, I KNOW! ...WAS THAT REALLY YUICHIRO-KUN?
He seemed possessed or something.
HUFF
HUFF
I HATE TO SAY IT, BUT...
...YEAH, HE'S REALLY LIKE THAT. HE'S SÔ-CHAN'S BEST FRIEND, AFTER ALL.
Since they were five years old.

SLURP
WELL... I LIKE SEEING THAT HE CAN GET A LITTLE AGGRESSIVE IN THE SUMMER HEAT, YOU KNOW? ♡
Huh...
TH-THUMP TH-THUMP
...
YEAH, I KIND OF DO, TOO...
ZAP!
ACK!
I KNOW MINA ISN'T A ROBOT, BUT...
...I SWEAR I SAW LASERS SHOOT OUT OF HER EYES.
D-DON'T FREAK OUT! MY HEART BELONGS TO SÔ-KUN, OKAY?
BAM
GOOD. IF YOU SWITCH TO YU-CHAN, I CAN'T PROMISE YOU'LL LIVE.
UNDERSTOOD!

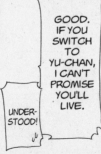

WITH THIS BODY AND THIS SUIT, I'M GONNA EAT YU-CHAN FOR LUNCH!
WHOA...!
I GOTTA GIVE HER CREDIT ...
...SHE REALLY GOES FOR IT.
I...
I'M GOING TO TELL SÔ-KUN HOW I FEEL TODAY !!
I'm sorry, Yu-chan, but I don't want any misunder-standings.
IN THIS KIND OF HEAT, BRAINS DON'T WORK PRO-PERLY. YOU MIGHT WANT TO CUT TO THE CHASE AND LEAVE THE CON-FESSION FOR PILLOW TALK.
DEAL!
YOU REALLY ARE A BEAST, AREN'T YOU...?
TEE HEE!
SIT STILL!

I'VE GOT TO HIDE THAT BRUISE.
HA HA!
IT TICK-LES!
...
WHAT ?
STARTLED
WHAT ...?
IF YOU WANNA SAY SOME-THING, SAY IT.
HE'S ACTING WEIRD ...
UM...
IT'S NOTH-ING.

OKAY, LINE UP...

WATCH THAT YOU DON'T TRIP! AND THE BOUNCE BOARD MIGHT BE A BIT BRIGHT, BUT KEEP YOUR EYES OPEN, OKAY?

CLICK

FLASH

SIGH...

SPLASH

IS IT OKAY TO SWIM HERE? THE WAVES LOOK PRETTY ROUGH. WHAT DO YOU THINK?

I THINK YOU'D BE HARD-PRESSED TO FIND AN EMPTY BEACH THAT'S SAFE FOR SWIMMING.

CRASH
OOPS ...
WHOA!
THAT WAS CLOSE.
MY BARE BACK AGAINST HIS BELLY... SKIN-ON-SKIN...
THANKS. I'M FINE NOW. OKAY... OKAY?
I CAN'T HEAR YOU.
SQUEEZE

...OH.
I'M NOT SURE HOW TO FEEL ABOUT THIS. IT'S LIKE SOME CRAZY MIX OF HEAVEN AND HELL...!!
NO BOY HAS EVER SAID HE LOVED ME BEFORE... I USED TO THINK I'D FALL FOR ANYONE WHO'D FALL FOR ME.
FLOATING
NOW THERE'S THIS GREAT LOOKING GUY WHO WANTS ME, BUT...
BLAZE
THEN THE HELLISH PART COMES IN...

HOW DARE YOU, AI-AI ...?!
Fume Fume
SPLOOSH
HEY! SHE'LL GET CAUGHT IN THE UNDER-TOW!
GET HER!
MINA!
GAAAHH!!
GASP!
A SEA MON-STER ?!
CHOKE
AI-AI! DID YOU JUST PULL YOUR HAND AWAY?!
I-I'M SO SORRY !!
AAAAHH!!!
THAT'S IT! THAT'S ENOUGH. CHANGE INTO THE LAST LOOK AND LET'S WRAP THIS UP!

PATTER PAT
SÔ-KUN!
WHAT? SHOULDN'T YOU BE CHANGING?
Girls take longer than guys, right?
UM ... WELL ...
HE'S... HE'S ACTING LIKE NOTHING HAPPENED ...
YEAH ...
I'M BREAKING INTO A COLD SWEAT...
I GOTTA SAY SOMETHING. ANYTHING...

YUICHIRO-KUN ISN'T THE ONE I'M INTER-ESTED IN... I HAVE A CRUSH ON *YOU,* SÔ-KUN.
I-I SAID IT!!
GRIN

YEAH, WELL, YOU CAN SAY IT...
...BUT I DON'T HAVE TO CELEBRATE.
CRASH...
QUIVER
QUIVER

YUICHIRO IS LIKE A BROTHER TO ME, BUT THERE ARE SOME THINGS I DON'T PLAN TO SHARE.

HE... HE HATES ME...

I MUST NOT CRY. I MUST NOT CRY. I MUST NOT...

OKAY, ALL DONE!

YOU'RE IN A GOOD MOOD. PINK LOOKS GREAT ON YOU.
REALLY? YOU THINK SO?
GRIN
SO, AI-AI... HOW'D IT GO WITH SÔ-CHAN?
THAT? OH... IT WAS A COMPLETE DISASTER.
HA HA HA!
WHAT?!
AI-AI! SNAP OUT OF IT! YOU MUST NEVER GIVE UP!
MINA...
How sweet...
GRAB

SHAKE SHAKE
YOU MUST PERSEVERE! FOR MY SAKE! FOR YU-CHAN AND ME!!
TH-THIS GIRL ...!
I CAN'T GET UPSET. I DON'T WANT SO-KUN TO SEE ME CRY ANYMORE...
WELL, MINA, GET READY ...
I'M GONNA TELL YUICHIRO-KUN THAT I'M NOT INTERESTED IN DATING HIM.
HM...
BUSY DAY, HUH ...?
...REJECTING AND REJECTED. I'VE GOT TO HAND IT TO YOU, AI-AI. YOU'RE TOUGHER THAN I THOUGHT YOU WERE.
IF I WERE YOU, I'D BE A MESS.
YEAH, WELL ...

CLICK
OKAY, YOU'RE ALL ON BREAK...
...UNTIL TONIGHT, WHEN WE'LL SHOOT THE LOVERS. BE SURE AND PAIR UP--
--I'LL TAKE AI!
YOINK
"Ai," not "Ai-chan" ...?
!
WHATEVER. LET'S JUST GET THIS OVER WITH...
HEY!

DON'T YOU KNOW YOU'RE SUPPOSED TO ASK PER-MISSION WHEN YOU TAKE SOME-THING THAT BELONGS TO SOMEONE ELSE?
OH, NOW SHE BE-LONGS TO YOU?
NOW THAT SOME-BODY ELSE WANTS HER?
SOME-BODY WHO CAN'T KEEP HIS GREEDY HANDS TO HIM-SELF.
WHOA! AAAH!
LET GO!
YOU LET GO!!
KICK
SPLISH
SPLASH
STOP! MY "LOVERS IN YUKATA" SET-UP...

...LOOKS MORE LIKE A "MURDER-SUICIDE... IN YUKATA"!!
LOCATION · JAPAN SEA
BLUBBLE...
C-CAN'T BREATHE ...
YOU'VE BEEN GETTING ON MY NERVES SINCE WE WERE FIVE!
HA! YOU BIG BABY! AI, TELL HIM!
NOOOO! I CAN'T AFFORD TO BUY THE YUKATA, TOO!
YOU ...
LET ME JOIN YOU!
... YOU'RE ALL...
...SO SELFISH...
H--
SNAP

SPLOOSH
HAVEN'T YOU EVER HEARD OF OOKA ECHIZEN ?!

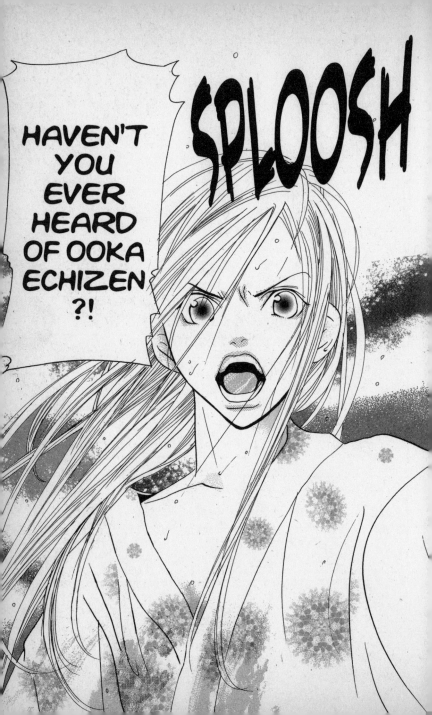

CRASH
EH?
OOKA ...?
Huff
Huff
JUDGE OOKA
TWO WOMEN CLAIMED THE SAME CHILD. JUDGE OOKA TOLD THEM TO EACH TAKE ONE OF THE CHILD'S ARMS AND PULL. WHEN ONE WOMAN SAW THE CHILD'S PAIN AND LET GO, HE KNEW THAT SHE WAS THE REAL MOTHER.
SNIFF...
HOW CAN YOU NOT KNOW THAT STORY? YOU DON'T CARE HOW I FEEL, DO YOU?
YOU'RE FIGHTING JUST TO FIGHT.
MY WHOLE LIFE I'VE BEEN RE-JECTED BY BOYS AND ALL I WANTED WAS A LITTLE ATTENTION ...

AND NOW THAT I HAVE TWO GOOD-LOOKING GUYS WHO ARE BOTH AFTER ME... I DON'T WANT EITHER ONE OF YOU!!

BOTH OF YOU CAN SHOVE IT!

THAT DOES IT...

UH OH! AI-AI!

SHE PASSED OUT.

OH? REALLY?!

Good one.

OHHH...

CLAP

CLAP

CLAP

CLAP

WOBBLE CLAP

CLAP

CLAP

CLAP

TWO WEEKS LATER ...
"EDO STYLE IS FRESH! WEAR A YUKATA LIKE AN ACTRESS IN A PERIOD PIECE..."
EDO STYLE IS FRESH!!
IT'S STUPID!! I CAN'T BELIEVE THEY FEATURED THIS.
HEY, AI-AI ...?
HA HA
LETHARGIC
Printers' proofs.
AH, MAN. INSTEAD OF GETTING SPOILED, SHE'S ROTTING IN THE SUMMER SUN...
I DON'T WANT TO SEE THEM. I'M SUCH AN IDIOT--WHAT WAS I THINKING...?
C'MON, CLASSES START TOMORROW. PERK UP.
I DON'T WANT TO GO.

YOU'RE MUM-BLING. I CAN'T HEAR YOU.

THAT'S RIGHT...

AI'S WORDS LIT A FIRE IN THE HEARTS OF TWO MEN WHO WERE MORE ACCUSTOMED TO LIGHTING FIRES THEM-SELVES.

BUT AI MAEKAWA WAS BORN UNDER AN UNLUCKY STAR, AND SO, NO MATTER HOW HARD SHE STRUGGLES, HER FATE IS A DIFFICULT ONE.

HER THORNY PASSAGE CONTINUES IN THE NEXT CHAPTER, AS WE GO... **BACK TO SCHOOL!**

You look like my dog, Blackie.
I HATED HIM RIGHT FROM THE START...

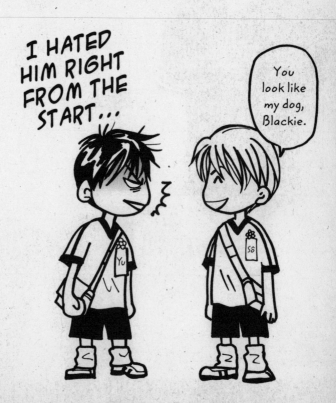

doubt!!

Chapter 7

ATARI
ATARI
REYES
REYES

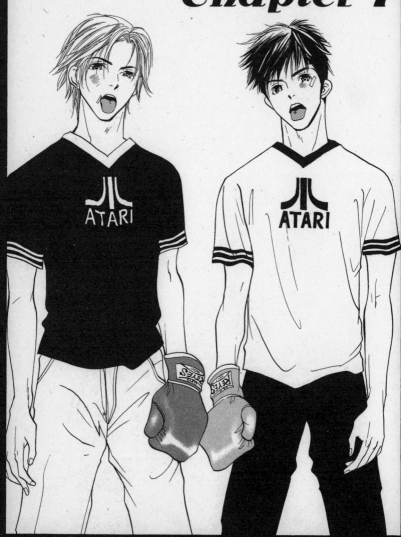

FLUTTER

MAYBE I SHOULD BECOME A NUN...

Sigh...

Quiver

JUST GIVE UP, YOU KNOW? I MEAN ...

...I WAS BORN UNDER A BAD STAR. I'LL NEVER HAVE A BOY-FRIEND.

... RIGHT?

Sô Ichinose

Before I even realized it was happening, Sô took on a life of his own. He isn't the kind of character I meant him to be. In Volume 3, I'll tell you more about his personal life. Keep reading!

I don't have a care in the world.

BOP
OUCH! MINA! THAT HURT!
HOW CAN YOU KEEP TALKING LIKE YOU'RE SOME KIND OF EXPERT ON MEN-- WHEN YOU HAVEN'T EVEN POPPED YOUR CHERRY?!
YOU'RE A FOOL, OKAY? YOU TURNED DOWN *TWO GUYS* WHEN THEY CAME AFTER YOU!
And they were both hot!
OUCH!
SNAP
WOMEN. NEED. MEN. MEN ARE LIKE VITAMINS, OKAY? YOU HAVE TO HAVE THEM. THAT'S THE LAW OF THE JUNGLE.
STAB
WELL, I DON'T LIVE IN THE JUNGLE!

HEE HEE ...
I GOT AI MAE-KAWA'S HAIR... ♡
WHAT THE --?!
SHUDDER
BAM
CRACK
CRACK
HEY ...

LONG TIME NO SEE, AI-CHAN.

SÔ... KUN.

IT... H-H-HURTS.

GRAB

WHAT WAS THAT FOR?!

YOU GUYS HEAR A DOG BARK-ING?

YOU CALLING ME A DOG?!

YES, I AM ...
ONLY A DOG WOULD BE DUMB ENOUGH TO BITE ME... RIGHT?
YOU OKAY?
YEAH... THANKS.
Whimper
YOU'RE PRETTY FAMOUS NOW, AI-CHAN. EVERYBODY SAW YOU IN THAT MAGAZINE OVER SUMMER BREAK.
ALL THE GUYS WANT A PIECE OF YOU NOW.
Better be careful.
Cool Steet
7
SIGH...
HE'S JUST AS HANDSOME AS EVER... ♡
FORGET IT! I'M NOT GOING THERE. HE'LL TORTURE ME FOR HIS OWN AMUSEMENT-- JUST LIKE THE LAST TIME. I'VE LEARNED MY LESSON.
I'M GOING TO THINK LIKE A *NUN!*
OH!
SQUINCH

MORNING, YU-CHAN!
Hey.
BUZZ BUZZ
THAT'S THE FAMOUS AI MAE-KAWA, HUH?
She's cute.
EXACTLY LIKE HER PHOTO. GET HER TO LOOK OVER HERE...
WHOA...
...WHAT'S WITH THE ARMED GUARDS?

HEY, DID ANYTHING HAPPEN BETWEEN THEM OVER THE SUMMER?
Hm. He can't help chasing...
...fleeing prey, I see.
THE TWO BEST GUYS! IT'S SO UNFAIR!
LONG TIME NO SEE, YUICHIRO-KUN. ♡ HOW'VE YOU BEEN?
I'M STILL HERE, AREN'T I?
HA HA! I HOPE SO! RIGHT, AI-CHAN?
INDEED. TEE HEE!
HA HA HA!
RATTLE
13HR
Huh?

WE ONLY HAVE A HALF-DAY TODAY, SO LET'S PUT YOUR DESKS BACK WHERE THEY BELONG AND GET STARTED, OKAY?
NO!
ISN'T IT WRITTEN IN THE STUDENTS' HAND-BOOK THAT...
BLAZING
...OUR FACULTY'S POLICY IS TO RESPECT STUDENT INITIA-TIVES?
THANK GOD!

Izumi's Family Portrait
Part 3
◀ Izumi's Brother ▶
Power Points: 800
Happiness Points: —2000
The Izumi family ties are all pretty loose, but this one is the loosest. In fact, it might already be severed.
I haven't seen him for six years now.
I wonder if he's still alive... If he were dead, wouldn't we get some kind of official notice?
Such indiffer-ence! I can't believe we're related.
mom
dad
Hey, Bro! Come home at least once while you're still in your 20s, okay?

HOW COME NO ONE WANTED ME WHEN I WANTED TO BE WANTED, HUH...? ONCE I GAVE UP...
Yuichiro, give up on Ai. Don't make me make you.
If you think you can ...!
Okay, kids ...
RIIING RIIING
DASH
NOW THAT THEY WANT ME, I CAN'T ENJOY IT! ♡
THE LAST TIME, I ALMOST DROWNED TO DEATH!
That sucked.
KER-CLANK

HUH ?!
Wait just a...
HEY, I GOT HER!
LET ME GO! WHAT'RE YOU DOING ?!
DON'T WORRY. WE'RE NOT GOING TO HURT YOU...
CLOSER
CLOSER
BLUE SCHOOL BADGE... THAT MEANS THEY'RE UPPERCLASS-MEN...
Uh oh...
They look like trouble ...

SORRY, BUT WE PROMISED TO SHOW YOU OFF TO SOME GUYS AT ANOTHER SCHOOL ...
YOU COME BY AFTER CLASS, AND WE'LL GET THOSE CUFFS OFF. OKAY?
THAT'S ALL. ♡
THEY'RE LYING!
SWISH
I CAN'T. I ALREADY HAVE PLANS AFTER SCHOOL!
FOR WHAT? A CROSS-CHOP-ATTACK?
YOU WANNA GO SEE SOME WRESTING? WE'LL TOTALLY TAKE YOU.
IT'S NO GOOD. THEY'RE NOT LISTENING.
HI-YAH!
KICK

Huff
Huff
I TOLD YOU TO BE CAREFUL, AI... SEE?
ASSHOLE! WHAT WAS THAT?!
IT WAS A SMACKDOWN!
YOU CAN'T JUST JUMP SOMEBODY WITHOUT WARNING!
That's not how it works!
WE'RE KANTO BOYS. WE DON'T PLAY BY YOUR RULES!*
SHIFT
SHIFT
UM...

*Kanto is a region that is typified by Tokyo (the modern capital city) and its environs. Kato can tell by the other boy's accent that he's from Kansai, typified by the more reserved, traditional Kyoto (the old capital).

ARE YOU NOT *MEN?!* FIGHT!!

MINA ...!
SORRY!
I WANTED TO SAY SOME-THING LIKE THAT JUST ONCE ...
WHAM
POP
WHAT DO WE DO NOW?
WOW... A FREE-FOR-ALL ...
STAFF
STAFF
STAFF
HEY!! WHAT'S GOING ON OVER THERE ?!
OH, CRAP-- TEACH-ERS!
WE'RE GONNA PAY YOU AN OFFICIAL VISIT LATER! GOT THAT, ASSHOLES ?!

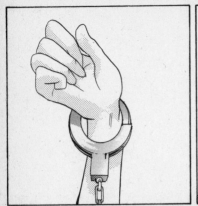

AN OFFICIAL VISIT? I'M SO HONORED!
ARE WE SUPPOSED TO STICK AROUND AND WAIT?
Fat chance.
UH...
CLINK
IT'S NO GOOD ...
13HR
I CAN'T GET IT OFF...
I GUESS I'D BETTER APOLOGIZE TO THOSE GUYS AND GET THE KEY, THEN...
NO WAY! WE NEED SOME SORT OF TOOL...
!
HAIR REMOVER FOAM
WHAT'S THAT?
MAYBE IF WE GREASE HER UP WITH THIS, SHE COULD SLIP HER HAND OUT...?
SHHWAA

WOW, IT STINKS!! THAT SHOULD BE CONSIDERED AIR POLLUTION!
WHY DO WOMEN BOTHER WHEN THEY'RE NOT EVEN HAIRY?
Don't tell him...
No way ...
HAVE YOU EVER HEARD OF "WAXING"? IT'S LIKE RIPPING HAIR OUT WITH DUCT TAPE.
RIIIP
GAH! IT HURTS JUST THINKING ABOUT IT.
DON'T GUYS PREFER SMOOTH SKIN?
WHO LOOKS AT ARMS AND LEGS?
Other parts, sure...
BANISH EXCESS HAIR!
BEFORE
AFTER
WHAAAT?! THAT'S A HORRIBLE THING TO SAY! WE WORK SO HARD!
DO YOU HAVE ANY IDEA HOW MANY HUNDREDS OF THOUSANDS WE SPEND ON SKIN CARE?!

...WELL, I GUESS IF YOU'RE GONNA DO IT, IT'S BETTER THAN SHAVING.
WHEN A GIRL HAS SERIOUS STUBBLE, IT CAN MAKE THE SEX PRETTY UNPLEA-SANT.
SEE, THAT'S WHY!
HA HA HA!
SEE? HE TORTURES ME ON PURPOSE.
Who was this stubbly girl...?
Uh...
FORGET IT. JUST GIVE ME YOUR HAND...
CLASP
OH...
JERK

...WHAT?
I...I DON'T KNOW...
TAP
ALL DAY, I'VE THOUGHT...
...THAT YOU WERE TRYING TO KEEP YOUR DIS-TANCE.
AM I IMAGIN-ING IT?

SHE DOESN'T HAVE TO EXPLAIN HERSELF TO YOU...
...SHE'S NOT YOUR GIRL-FRIEND.
SURE SHE IS. I DECIDED.
YOU THINK THAT'S HOW IT WORKS?
I DO.
I--

I CAN'T KEEP UP WITH YOU, SÔ-KUN.
WHEN I TOLD YOU HOW I FELT, YOU BLEW ME OFF. AND NOW...
I DON'T UNDER-STAND YOU. AND I... I JUST CAN'T KEEP UP.
THUNK
... SÔ!
SÔ-CHAN, THE HAND-CUFFS--
WHY SHOULD I BOTHER? SHE'S NOT MY *GIRL-FRIEND* AFTER ALL.

THERE YOU ARE.

CRUNCH

MINA'S LOOKING FOR YOU. SHE WANTS TO GRAB A BITE ON THE WAY HOME.

I GUESS THAT'S HER WAY OF SHOWING SHE CARES.

SÔ'S ALREADY GONE, SO YOU CAN TELL ME...

...ARE YOU OKAY WITH THIS?

...YEAH...

WHAT AM I SAYING?! OF COURSE I'M NOT OKAY WITH IT!!
I'M CRAZY ABOUT HIM! LOOK AT THE WAY HE PROTECTS ME! I'VE BEEN IN LOVE WITH HIM SINCE OUR FIRST DAY... IT'S JUST...
"...HE'S NUTS"?
NOD
HE'S TOO MUCH FOR ME...
IT'S LIKE I CAN SEE HOW I'LL GET HURT... AND I'M SCARED.
SNIFF...
WHAT DO YOU WANT FROM HIM, THEN?

I WANT HIM TO LOVE ME AS MUCH AS I LOVE HIM...
...AND TO BE GENTLE AND SINCERE...
...AND NO MATTER HOW MANY YEARS GO BY, FOR EVERYONE AROUND US TO ENVY US...
...AND I WANT HIM TO BUY ME AN ORCHID ON MY BIRTHDAY EVERY YEAR.
GUYS LIKE THAT DON'T EXIST!
I KNOW THAT!!
BUT I DON'T WANT TO BELIEVE IT!!
WO-MEN...
Impos-sible...!
RUSTLE
WAIT, SÔ TOLD ME...

...THAT WOMEN ARE VULNER-ABLE AT TIMES LIKE THESE...
"WHEN SHE'S HAVING TROUBLE WITH HER MAN, SHE NEEDS A STRONG SHOUL-DER TO CRY ON, YOU KNOW...? JUST GO FOR IT!!"
You...!!
"JUST GO FOR IT!!"
"GO!!"
AI...
IF YOU WANT SÔ THAT BADLY, DON'T BE STUBBORN !!

I THINK... YOU'VE STILL GOT A CHANCE.
YUICHIRO-KUN ...
WHAT A NICE GUY... I COULD FALL FOR HIM...
CLASP
HA HA ...
I'D HATE MYSELF IF I TOOK SÔ'S ADVICE !!
DAMMIT!!
YU-CHAN! AI-AI!
RUN! GO!!
BE-HIND YOU!!

GATHER
THERE THEY ARE ...
AN OFFICIAL VISIT, JUST LIKE WE PROMISED ...
GATHER
BOLT
C'mon!
AAAH! I TOTALLY FORGOT ABOUT THEM!
THERE'S A WHOLE ARMY!
BOLT
AI-CHAN, GO INSIDE AND HIDE WHILE I HOLD THEM OFF!
Thanks, Yuichiro-kun!
PAT
PAT
PAT
PA
WHY DOES THIS KIND OF THING ALWAYS HAPPEN TO ME...?
SOME-BODY... HELP...

PBBLT!

SÔ-KUN!
HE HASN'T
GONE
HOME
YET.

WHAT?! HE'S NOT NUTS, HE'S...
...A BIG BABY!!
DASH
SHE'S TRYING TO GET HELP FROM THAT GUY!
GET HER!
DASH
DASH
DASH
HOW...
...COULD I HAVE FALLEN...
... FOR SOME-ONE LIKE THAT?

SMACK

HUH?

I'M IN TROUBLE, AND YOU JUST *WATCH*...? WHAT KIND OF MAN ARE YOU?
Huff
Huff
OUCH!
...THE KIND WHO'S NOT GOING TO RISK HIS NECK FOR SOMEBODY ELSE'S GIRL.
THAT IS *WRONG* !!
Y-YOU GUYS... NOT A LOVERS' QUARREL ...
Please!
THAT'S JUST WHO I AM. THERE'S NOTHING WE CAN DO ABOUT THAT.
LET ME BE VERY CLEAR ABOUT THIS:
I don't want you anymore.
KER CLANK

WHAT ?!
WHAT IS THIS ?!
YANK
DON'T MESS AROUND! GET IT OFF!

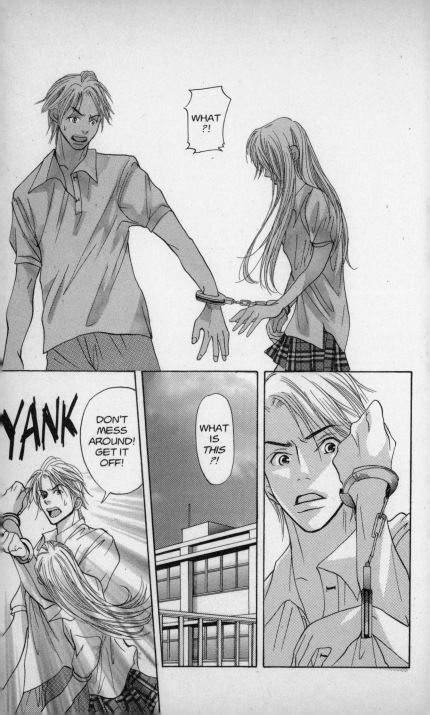

GET THIS THING--

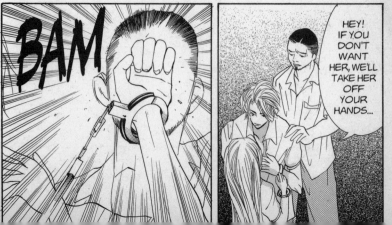

HEY! IF YOU DON'T WANT HER, WE'LL TAKE HER OFF YOUR HANDS...

BAM

DASH

GAH!

SIGH...

ER ...

I CAN'T BELIEVE I LET YOU *TRAP* ME...

FLOAT

BLUSH

I MEAN, HOW THE HELL ...?

DASH DASH DASH
YUICHI-RO!
SÔ!
LEAVE HIM!
Let's go!
IT WAS A LONG AND THORNY ROAD...
...BUT IT'S ABOUT TO COME TO AN END.
AI-CHAN, YOU ARE ...
WHAT...? TELL ME.
...AND NOW, OUR LIFE TOGETHER CAN BEGIN!

TOO HEAVY!
What do you weigh?
...AND END ...
TICK
...IN ALL OF 0.01 SECONDS !!
TICK
YOU'RE HORRIBLE! TOO HORRIBLE! I'LL BE A NUN, I TELL YOU!
YOU WEIGH A *TON?*
SEE, AI-CHAN? THAT'S WHY YOU SHOULD DATE ME INSTEAD.
HER THORNY PASSAGE CONTINUES...
...AND AS LONG AS AI MAEKAWA IS IN LOVE WITH SÔ ICHINOSE, THAT ROAD WILL NEVER END. SOMEHOW, SHE DOESN'T REALIZE...

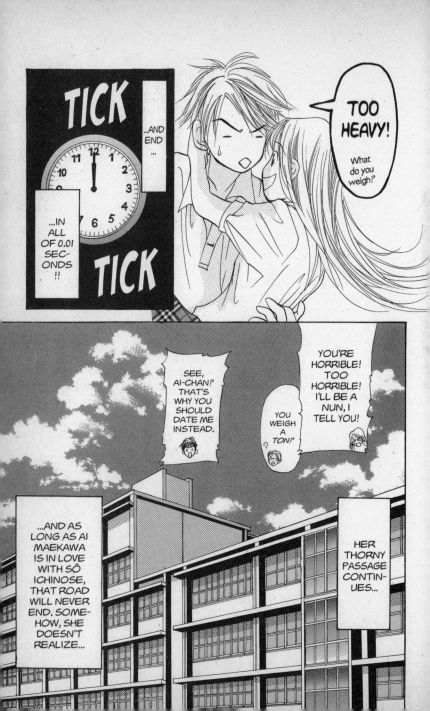

EVERY NOW AND THEN, I WONDER HOW MUCH MONEY HAIR REMOVAL MODELS MUST GET PAID...

(Especially the Western girls...)

Hair-Free Beauty!

Chapter 8

doubt!!

BACK BEFORE I WAS PRETTY...
...IT SEEMED LIKE BOYS WERE FROM ANOTHER PLANET.
I ENVIED THE GIRLS WHO COULD JUST CHAT WITH THEM CASUALLY.
HA HA HA!
Seriously?
SO I WAS WATCHING THIS COP SHOW LAST NIGHT...
I SAW THAT SHOW!
I'll join in...!
HUH?
Did she say some-thing?
1 MILLION LIGHT YEARS

Mina Sato

When I first started this series, I didn't plan to make her as important as she's become... Now, she's a regular. I just need to convince her to do something about that out-of-control tan...

Humans are animals, too.

HEH...
IT'S OKAY! THE BOYS IN MY CLASS AREN'T THAT GREAT, ANY-WAY. I'VE GOT HIGH STAN-DARDS.
I'm holding out for a good one!
I MADE EXCUSES,
BUT...
...I THOUGHT I WAS DOOMED.
WAHH..
UNTIL ...!!
13HR
TOOK THEM LONG ENOUGH ...
THE MOST POPULAR GIRL AND THE MOST POPULAR BOY...
Sniff...
WHAT HAVE I GOT TO LIVE FOR NOW ...?

GOOD MORN-ING!
SPARKLE
SPARKLE
SPARKLE
SPARKLE
SPARKLE
SPARKLE
WOW. THAT COULD MAKE YOU GO BLIND...
MAN ...
I, AI MAEKAWA, AM FINALLY A WINNER !!
It's super! ♡♥
Heh...

MINA, AS A WOMAN, I CAN TELL YOU IT'S A BAD IDEA TO SPEND YOUR SUMMER BREAK MOPING...
...
She's worse than before ...
SUDDENLY YOU'RE AN EXPERT? AT LEAST I GOT SOME THIS SUMMER...
WELL, WE'VE BEEN THROUGH A LOT, BUT IT'S ALL BEEN WORTH IT...
IF THERE'S ANY WAY I CAN HELP YOU IN THAT DEPARTMENT, FEEL FREE TO ASK...
FAR-AWAY EYES
YOU'RE SUCH A LITTLE GIRL, AI-AI.
WHO IS HE?
He's hot.
HAYATA-SAN... HE'S IN COLLEGE. WE BANGED ONCE-- BIG TIME.
B-BANGED?! WAIT, JUST LIKE THAT...?
No modesty ...?
PFFT!
Heh...
You banged--

WHAT?! HOW DARE SHE...?!
Am I...?
SIGH...
THAT WEARY, WISTFUL SIGH... IT'S SO UNLIKE HER...
YU-CHAN DOESN'T CARE ABOUT ME, AND I JUST COULDN'T STAND TO HAVE A MAN-FREE SUMMER.
BUT WE ONLY DID IT ONCE, AND I HAVEN'T HEARD FROM HIM SINCE... I WAS SURE THAT MY TECH--
WHAT TECHNIQUE?!
Virgin. Totally interested.

TECH-NIQUE ...?
What?
JUMP
I'M LOSING MY FAITH IN WO-MEN...
WANNA SWITCH TO MEN? YUICHIRO, THE NEXT TIME I SEE YOU, YOU COULD BE A DIFFERENT MAN...
GUFFAW
Sorry about that, Yuichiro...
HM ...
THE UNIVER-SITY IS NEARBY...
I could stop by on my way home...
WAIT!

WHY WOULD I GO CHECK OUT THE GUY MINA SLEPT WITH...?
THAT'S WEIRD, RIGHT?
Bad idea.
She brought the photo.
ANY MAN WHO RAVISHES A GIRL AND THEN ABANDONS HER ISN'T WORTH IT.
I'D DO IT WITH SOME-ONE I LOVED, BUT I'D TAKE MY TIME...
WOOOOO
IF YOU WAIT TOO LONG, IT'LL ROT OFF!
Scary old spinster!
FLAIL
I'M NOT LIKE THAT ANY-MORE! GO AWAY!
POOF!
FLUTTER

HEY, HAYATA... THAT GIRL DROPPED A PICTURE OF YOU.
EEP!
HAVE WE MET...?
DAMN, I LIKE THAT UNIFORM.
Sexy.
SHE'S CUTE, HAYATA. INTRODUCE US! ♡
I DON'T EVEN KNOW HER!
MAYBE SHE'S STALKING YOU!!
Huh? No...
YOU SERIOUS?!
THAT'S NOT IT! I JUST WANT AN EXPLANATION...

* "Cotteria" -- a spoof on the name of a popular fast food restaurant in Japan.

*
コッテリア
HAMBURGERS
YOU JUST WANTED TO TALK TO ME ABOUT YOUR FRIEND?
YES ...
AM I ACTING LIKE A BUSY-BODY?
This isn't what I intended at all.

I CAN'T BE RESPON-SIBLE FOR EVERY GIRL I BANG... YOU KNOW WHAT I'M SAYIN'? I MEAN... WOMEN WANT ME. WHO AM I TO REFUSE THEM?
So what?!
YOU'RE NOT VERY NICE TO MINA...
DON'T YOU LOVE HER AT ALL?
He makes me MAD!
YOU DON'T THINK I DO, DO YOU?
PUFF

IT'S NOT LIKE HIGH SCHOOL GIRLS TODAY DON'T HAVE SEX WITHOUT COMMITMENT ALL THE TIME, YOU KNOW?
WHAT?
WHAT?
ACK!! WHAT'S THE MATTER?! C'MON! YOU'RE COOL, AREN'T YOU?!
DO I LOOK COOL ...?!
LOOK, I DON'T KNOW WHAT YOU'RE AFTER, BUT...
STUB
...I ALREADY HAVE A GIRL-FRIEND.
SO IT'S NO USE DECLARING YOUR LOVE FOR ME.

ROARRR!!
WHO THE HELL DOES HE THINK HE IS?
RIIING RIIING
AI-CHAN'S BEEN BLOWING UP ALL DAY.
SHE'S MAD ABOUT WHAT HAPPENED YESTER-DAY...
THAT'S MINA'S BUSI-NESS, ISN'T IT?
I AGREE. YOU SHOULD STAY OUT OF IT.
SÔ-KUN AND YUICHIRO-KUN, TOO...! MEN ARE COLD.

HE USED HER FOR SEX! AM I THE ONLY ONE WHO CARES?
...
FUMING ...
...AI, HAVE YOU EVER HEARD SHINGEN TAKEDA'S* TREATISE ON WO-MEN?
HE SAID HUNT YOUR PREY AS FAST AS FIRE, HOLD HER AS FIRM AS THE MOUNTAINS ...
CIVIL WAR ERA
TOSS YOUR SPEAR IN WOODS, AND THEN RUN AS FAST AS THE WIND.
HIT & AWAY!
REMEM-BER: "FIRE· MOUN-TAINS· WOODS· WIND"
HEY, SÔ-CHAN ...
SMACK!
OUCH. WHEN DID YOU GET HERE?
13 HR
I'VE BEEN HERE THE ENTIRE TIME!!
I'm in the same class as you!

* http://www.samurai-archives.com/shingen.html

BUT... SERI-OUSLY, I'M NOT SO SURE ABOUT THAT HAYATA GUY.
SNUB
I KNOW... I HEARD HE WAS WITH ANOTHER WOMAN YESTER-DAY...
SHE'S SUP-POSEDLY A STUDENT HERE.
SERI-OUSLY?! THAT'S UNFOR-GIVABLE! THE WOMAN, TOO!
--WAIT... ACTUALLY, THAT WAS ME.
Yesterday
WHO ARE YOU?! AFTER YU-CHAN...? MUST YOU TAKE ALL MY MEN?
IT WASN'T LIKE THAT! JUST FORGET ABOUT THAT GUY THOUGH, OKAY?!
I wasn't yours to steal.
YOU'RE THE ONE WHO KEEPS BRING-ING HIM UP!

BESIDES... HOW AM I SUPPOSED TO FORGET ?!
POOR MINA... MAYBE SHE'S REALLY IN LOVE WITH HIM.
IT'S SO UNLIKE HER ...
SO WHAT IF SHE IS?
C'MON...
LET'S NOT TALK ABOUT MINA WHEN WE'RE ALONE.

ULP
WE'RE ALONE!
RUSTLE RUSTLE
THE EARLY STAGE OF A RELATION-SHIP IS CRUCIAL! I DON'T WANT HIM TO THINK I'M BORING...
Er... Um...
DID YOU SEE THAT COP SHOW LAST NIGHT?
HUH?
THIS ISN'T GOING SO WELL.
Hm...
OH, ON TV? NO, BUT I SAW...
HUH?
Did you say some-thing?

THIS IS TER-RIBLE!
IT'S JUST THE SAME AS BE-FORE!!
ERM--
AHH... SHE'S JUST LIKE A STRAY CAT...
ERM--
ERM--
It wants the treat, but it's too scared to come closer.
ERM--
ERM--
AI...

HA HA!
SQUEEZE
K--
EEEEEK!!
KISSING?! WHAT DO I DO?!
EYES! AM I SUPPOSED TO CLOSE MY EYES? HANDS! WHERE AM I SUPPOSED TO PUT MY GIANT HANDS?!
EEEEEK!!

I SHOULD'VE ASKED MINA ...
Mwah!
In Sô's mind.
MINA COULD HAVE ...
TREMBLE TREMBLE
WIND
FIRE
WOODS
MOUNTAINS
...AND I HAVEN'T HEARD FROM HIM SINCE.
WAIT A SECOND !!
AN UNMARRIED WOMAN CAN'T DO THIS! I BET IN SOME RELIGIONS IT'S CONSIDERED A CRIME...
I'M A BUDDHIST. YOU?
CRUNCH
JUST KISS HIM ALREADY, WILL YOU?

HER NAIVETÉ IS ADORABLE, ISN'T IT?
IT'S LAME, IF YOU ASK ME.
WH-WHY'RE YOU HERE?!
WE WERE JUST PASSING BY...
HE'S SO CLOSE AND INSTEAD OF GOING TO SEE MINA, HE'S OUT WITH ANOTHER WOMAN.
LEAVE US ALONE!
Idiot!
MINA IS A FOOL TO FALL FOR A MAN LIKE THAT!!
HAYATA!
IT'S A CRIME TO STOP HIM ONCE YOU'VE GONE THAT FAR!

WE'RE NOT LIKE YOU! WE DON'T GO AROUND BRAGGING ABOUT HOW MANY PEOPLE WE'VE SLEPT WITH!
WE'RE SATISFIED WITH THE TYPE OF RELATIONSHIP RECOMMENDED BY THE BOARD OF EDUCATION! RIGHT, SÔ-KUN?
HUH...? WHAT?
Draw...
WOW, SMELLS LIKE VIRGINS.
...IT STINKS.

Izumi's Family Portrait

Part 4

◀ Myself ▶

Power Points: — 2000
Hopelessness: ∞
(Impossible to measure)

Every now and then, **I wonder why I'm alive,** and suddenly, in the middle of the night, I cannot help acting like a monkey.

Oo ah ah!
Oo oo!
Gone wild due to violent nervous tension.

Naturally, the fact that I'm alive puzzles me... and that puzzlement depresses me...

AHH
...

GRR
GRR
GRR
...I'M ABOUT TO LOSE IT.
HOW ABOUT YOU, AI?
...
...
Baby, let's check out, so that I can check in... inside you.
You silly...
SMACK
高
入口
時間

WHERE TO? THIS CAR IS PRETTY FAST, YOU KNOW.
SNOW BRAND MILK
SPLASH
WHA--?!
The windshield!
SQUEAK SQUEAK
WHAT THE HELL?! THE WIPERS ARE MAKING IT WORSE!
WATER ...
THAT WON'T WORK ...
The milk fat is like grease.
OH WELL, GUESS YOU WON'T BE ABLE TO DRIVE SINCE YOU CAN'T SEE...

THAT WAS WHOLE MILK, OF COURSE.
I HAVE NO QUALMS ABOUT VANDALIZING THAT 3 SERIES* YOUR PARENTS BOUGHT YOU.
BURST
YOU FREAKS ...!
CHOMP
AAHHHHH!!
AWESOME! JUST LIKE OBA Q!*
HEE HEE
WILL YOU PLEASE GIVE MY DOG BACK?
0824

※ BMW.

* "Oba Q" from the anime *Obake no Q-taro* is scared of dogs... because dogs like to bite him.

DASH

Who is this ...?

I'LL KILL YOU !!

YES ...

no

DO YOU REMEMBER THIS DAY? DID HE TELL YOU HE'D BE MEETING A FRIEND OR SOMETHING?

OKAY!

LET'S SPLIT UP!

IDIOTS! OF COURSE I'LL GO AFTER THE WOMAN.

Duh!

DASH
DASH
DASH

NO! DON'T! WAAAH!
WHY MUST YOU FOLLOW ME EVERY DAY?
WAH! WAH!
WHAT ?!
WILL YOU PLEASE STOP? PLEASE!
EVERY DAY ...?
HE'S A STALK-ER?
BUZZ BUZZ
NO WAY! DISGUST-ING!
HIS PANTS ARE FILTHY. CALL THE POLICE!
IT WAS THE DOG!
IT'S NOT WHAT YOU THINK!
カラオケボックス
VBBBRR
CALL FROM SO-CHAN

PIP
SÔ-CHAN ...?
RIGHT NOW? BUT--
I'M STILL AT SCHOOL.
JUST COME OVER LIKE I SAID.
He's getting away.
Grab him!
I'VE GOT A PRE-SENT FOR YOU...
TRIP

IT'S A WILD DOG... A COL-LEGE CANINE.
HOW 'BOUT IT?
WHOA! WHAT'RE YOU DOING?!
ROUGH-ING HIM UP!
I'LL DO MORE! MAKE HIM CRY!!
HEE HEE
ACK!
AI-AI, STOP HIM!
NO WAY!

THAT GUY DE-SERVES IT!
HE HAD A GIRL-FRIEND THE WHOLE TIME!
...I ALREADY KNEW THAT.

MINA...

WHO CARES?! JUST FOR- GET IT.

I—

I'M SORRY. I THOUGHT YOU WERE... THE KIND OF GIRL WHO FOOLS AROUND WITH ANYONE.

THAT'S OKAY. I AM!
NO, IT'S NOT OKAY...
COULD WE START OVER AGAIN?
AS IF WE'D JUST MET...?
IT'S NOT JUST PHYSICAL! HE DOES CARE...
C'MON MINA, STOP CRYING...
MRF...
SHAKE
SHAKE

HA HA HA
BWA HA HA HA! NO WAY!
"AS IF WE'D JUST MET?" WHERE'D YOU GET THAT?! THAT'S HILARI-OUS!
HA HA
WHO'D WANT TO START OVER WITH YOU?
NO THANKS! PTOOEY!

REALLY, I NEVER CARED ABOUT HIM ...
SO WHAT IF HE HAD A GIRL-FRIEND ?
WHAT BOTHERED ME WAS THAT IT LOOKED LIKE HE USED ME... WHEN, IN REALITY, I USED HIM.
BUT... MINA, YOU SAID YOU COULD NEVER FORGET ...!
I COULDN'T! YOU KNOW HOW THAT MAKES ME LOOK?!
That's why I was depressed.
AI-AI, IT'S TIME YOU LET GO OF YOUR ILLUSIONS ABOUT MEN AND WOMEN.
C'MON, LET'S GO HOME.
MINA ...
You...
PAT
AND SO ...

I TOLD YOU GUYS TO STAY OUT OF IT!
NOW THAT *THAT'S* OVER, I CAN PURSUE YU-CHAN UNRESER-VEDLY.
LET GO!
GAAAAH!
NEVER AGAIN WILL I FEEL SORRY FOR MINA...
Wiser words were never spoken.
AND I SHOULDN'T FIGHT HIM EVER AGAIN ...
NOW I KNOW HOW SCARY SHE CAN GET...

WHAT WERE YOU THINKING JUST NOW, SÔ-KUN?
13 HR
UH... I WAS THINKING HOW CUTE YOU LOOK. HA HA HA!
MEN AND WOMEN...
...ARE LIKE CREATURES FROM DIFFERENT PLANETS.
EVEN THOUGH AI MAEKAWA AND SÔ ICHINOSE APPEAR TO BE VERY MUCH IN LOVE...
...THEY'LL ENGAGE IN INTERPLANETARY WAR VERY SOON.
LET'S BE NICE FROM NOW ON.
OKAY.

TO BE CONTINUED IN **DOUBT!!** VOLUME 3!

DOUBT

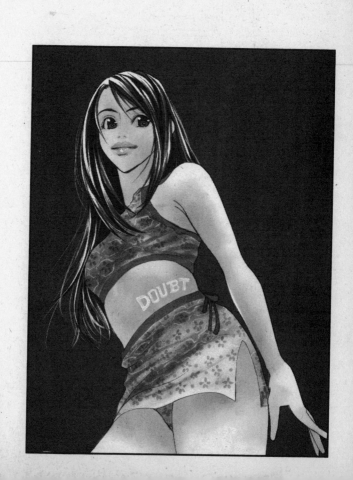

ORIGINAL MANGA FOR **DOUBT!!**
A SPECIAL EDITION OUTSIDE THE SERIES.

A WOMAN'S PATH

Yuichiro
Sô

Note: This early manga is very roughly drawn. Please read it with an uncritical mind!

DO YOU THINK THERE'S SUCH A THING AS HAVING "GENIUS FOR BEING A WOMAN"?
I THINK THERE IS...
IN EVERY CLASS, THERE'S ALWAYS ONE GIRL WHO SEEMS AVERAGE TO US, BUT SHE'S WILDLY POPULAR WITH BOYS.
I KNOW WHAT YOU MEAN... A WOMAN WHO'S POPULAR WITH MEN IS DIFFERENT FROM A WOMAN WHO'S POPULAR WITH WOMEN.
I DIDN'T ASK YOU.
CHIHARU ONLY CARES ABOUT BEING POPULAR WITH BOYS.
HEH ♥

Kyoka Mina Chiharu

(⇧Kyoka debuts in Vol. 3)

WHAT A HOR- RIBLE THING TO SAY...!

I DON'T THINK YOU GUYS UNDER- STAND THE BASICS.

BASICS ?

MEN !!

THAT'S LIFE.

MEN! MEN! *MEN!!* A WOMAN'S VALUE IS DETER- MINED BY THE CALIBER OF MAN SHE IS ABLE TO LAND!

IF OTHER WOMEN HATE HER FOR IT, SO BE IT!!

NOW... IF YOU WANT TO SNARE YOURSELF A GOOD MAN, I RECOM- MEND THE "FISH BOWL" TECHNIQUE...

FIND YOURSELF A BABY FISH WHO'S BOUND TO BECOME A GREAT BIG FISH, THEN PUT HIM IN A FISH BOWL CALLED YOURSELF, AND NURTURE HIM SLOWLY AND SURELY...
Sô, age 11 (baby fish)
BEFORE LONG, THE PROUD MOMENT COMES WHEN THAT BABY FISH IS EXACTLY THE GREAT BIG FISH YOU WANTED! ♡♡
EW! THAT'S WHAT MIDDLE-AGED MEN DO!
Hikaru Genji complex, right?*
WHY BOTHER? GREAT BIG FISH SWIM RIGHT UP TO ME.
FURIOUS
I THINK OF IT MORE LIKE HUNTING THAN FISHING ...
WHAT? YOU GIRLS HAVE TOO MUCH ENERGY. YOU COULD BREAK A LION'S NECK.
SHUT UP, YOU HAG!! I'M NOT BARBARIC.
THE SMARTER THE PREY, THE FASTER HE CAN RUN.
EVERY TIME I GET CLOSE, HE FINDS A WAY TO ESCAPE.
It's about time you gave up.

* In *The Tale of Genji,* older man Hikaru Genji tries to mold a young girl into the perfect wife.

BUT WHEN I FINALLY TAKE HIM DOWN, CAN YOU IMAGINE WHAT THAT CONQUEST WILL FEEL LIKE?
THRILL THRILL
UH... I THINK I KNOW HOW THAT FEELS. BUT ONCE YOU'VE HAD HIM, DON'T YOU GET BORED?
NOPE... NOT AT ALL...
BECAUSE I DEVOUR EVERY BIT... INCLUDING THE BONES.
THAT'S WHY THEY CALL IT THE KING-DOM OF THE WILD.
You beast.
PUFF
FOR YOU TWO, THE WORLD REVOLVES AROUND MEN.
THAT DOESN'T WORK FOR ME. I AM MY OWN MASTER.
HER MAJESTY THE QUEEN
YOU MUST UNDER-STAND THE *COMMERCE* OF LOVE. ANALYZE WITH A COOL HEAD EACH MAN'S ASSETS AND LIABILITIES...

SMART WOMEN CAN DATE WITHOUT HANDING OVER THE KEYS TO THE KING-DOM...
THE QUEEN WILL BE LEFT WITH THE SERVANTS, DON'T YOU THINK?
Good-bye, Kyoka-san!
Ha Ha!
THAT WON'T DO FOR US... WE'D RATHER DATE KINGS AND KNIGHTS.
BUT...
THERE ARE WOMEN WHO ARE JUST "AVERAGE," AND YET, SOMEHOW, THEY WIN.
HM? I WON-DER IF SHE'LL WIN IN THE END...?
I'LL SEE YOU AGAIN IN DOUBT!! VOLUME 3! ♡
WHAT ?
THE END

Thanks to you,

DOUBT!!, which we thought
would end by Volume 4, is still going--
so don't give up on us now.
Please read Volume 3, too.
If you buy it, you'll find my ♡love♡ inside.

In Vol. 3, 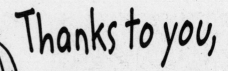 will
reveal himself, too!♡
(That sounds dirty, huh...?)

So, please continue
to support **Doubt!!**

The manga essays that follow

previously appeared in a
travel magazine called
Chikyu Komachi
("Small-Town Earth")
as well as in
Bessatsu Shôjo Comics.

They pretty much tell
you what an idiot I am,
but if you have the time,
you might as well
read them.

TRAVEL ESSAY

HAINAN ISLAND, THE HAWAII OF CHINA!

Yeah!

FELINE IQ

HERE WE GO!!

RESORT! VACATION! THE SCENT OF THE SUMMER LAND MAKES MY HEART DANCE!

I'M NOT SURE IF I'M QUALIFIED TO GO ON A TRIP WHERE I'M SUPPOSED TO WRITE UP A REPORT... OH WELL, IT'S OKAY! I'M A FOOL, AND THERE ARE FOOLS ALL OVER THE WORLD!

World Wide Fools?

AW...

I WAS EXCITED, BUT I KNEW VERY LITTLE CHINESE...

BU YAO = I DON'T WANT IT

MEI YOU = I DON'T HAVE IT

WO BU DONG = I DON'T UNDERSTAND

...JUST THOSE THREE PHRASES.

I MADE IT TO HAINAN ISLAND, AND...

IT WAS EXTREMELY HOT! LIKE A SAUNA!

No~

STEAM

S-SAN, THE CAMERA-MAN WHO GETS SWEATY EASILY, WAS IN REAL TROUBLE.

HE'S MELT-ING...

Editor Y-san

Writer T-san

WHOA!!

...

BECAUSE OF THE TROPICAL CLIMATE, YOU CAN BE IN CHINA, AND NOT FEEL LIKE YOU'RE IN CHINA...

Herd of water buffalo.

OHHH, THERE ARE GOATS! GOATS!
INDEED, THERE ARE MANY, MANY DIFFERENT ANIMALS (ALL DOMESTICATED).
IT'S LIKE THE KINGDOM OF MUTSUGORO!!*
DUCKS!
A HORSESHOE CRAB!
I hear they're edible...
PLEASE DON'T.

*A TV show like *Animal Planet*, or *Mutual of Omaha's Wild Kingdom*

HONK HONK
THOUGH IT'S A RESORT AREA, IT'S NOT OVER-DEVELOPED AND WE CAN STILL ENJOY FRESH, CLEAN AIR.
The water buffalo look pretty funny when they lie around obstructing traffic.

THE KIDS IN TOWN ARE SO CUTE!! THEIR EYES TWINKLE LIKE STARS.
I'M NOT USUALLY THAT INTERESTED IN KIDS, BUT I WANTED TO HUG THEM ALL...

SUPER-DEVELOPED RESORTS ARE PRETTY, BUT THEY FEEL ARTIFICIAL.
WHEN THERE ARE MORE TOURISTS THAN LOCALS, IT'S TOTALLY LAME.

WHEN I VISITED GUAM AND SAIPAN, I WAS SURROUNDED BY SO MANY OTHER JAPANESE TOURISTS THAT IT FELT AS IF I'D NEVER LEFT JAPAN!
AAAAAAAA!!
Japanese turning into zombies only interested in brands.
DFS
PUCCI!!
GUCCI!!

HAINAN ISLAND IS A DIFFERENT KIND OF RESORT! I RECOMMEND...
...THE SCENERY! IT'S BEAUTIFUL!! NO COMPLAINTS ABOUT IT. THE WATER IS ABSOLUTELY CRYSTAL-CLEAR.
THE NIGHT-LIFE IS ALSO WONDERFUL! IT'S GREAT TO TAKE A DIP IN THE POOL UNDER THE STARS!
AND THERE'S LIVE MUSIC IN THE HOTEL LOUNGE--WHAT MORE COULD WE ASK?
SPLASH
For some reason, Editor Y (age 33) had to practice diving. I wondered if he was playing some sort of game.
PLEASE VISIT OUR VILLAGES FOR FOLK ARTS AND CRAFTS.
OUR VILLAGES WILL REMIND YOU OF A THEME PARK.
One of the beautiful native Li people. ♡
AND THERE WAS THE SHOW...
HI-YAH!
IT WAS LIKE YOU WERE VISITING A STRANGE SCHOOL FESTIVAL, AND WITHOUT REALIZING IT, YOU GOT ROPED INTO DOING SOMETHING TOTALLY ALIEN.
...
...
...
...

WHAT ABOUT FOOD? SINCE IT'S AN ISLAND, LET'S EAT FRESH SEA-FOOD.
It's like a miniature marine museum.
You pick out the ingredients and get them prepared.
THESE WEIRD-LOOKING THINGS TURNED OUT TO BE WONDER-FULLY TASTY.
I THOUGHT THE SAVORY SEA URCHIN CUSTARD(?!) WAS THE BEST.
Using their shells as serving bowls. How cool!
SINCE I'M TALKING ABOUT FOOD, LET ME TELL YOU ABOUT A LITTLE CULTURE SHOCK I FELT!
AT THE FREE MARKETS IN CHINA, ALL KINDS OF ANIMALS ARE SOLD LIVE AS INGRE-DIENTS FOR DINNER. ESPECIALLY ...
THE JAPANESE LOVE THESE ANIMALS AS PETS. SO, IT WAS A SHOCKER.
KITTENS
PUPPIES
She's our guide in Guangzhou. Her name is Chin-san, and she's incredibly cute.
RED DOGS AND RED CATS ARE DELICIOUS. MEAT DOGS AND CATS ARE DIFFERENT FROM PET DOGS AND CATS.
The dogs and cats that people keep as pets don't taste very good.
How does she know?

APPARENTLY PEOPLE BUY A KITTEN, FOR EXAMPLE, AT THE CITY MARKET FOR A CERTAIN AMOUNT OF MONEY, AND THEN...
THIS ONE.
...THEY KEEP IT LIKE A PET FOR A WHILE UNTIL IT GETS BIGGER.
Don't feed it cat food. It'll make it taste bad.
ONCE YOU FEEL TOO ATTACHED TO EAT THE CAT, YOU TAKE IT TO THE CITY MARKET AND SELL IT TO SOMEONE ELSE, AND THEN BUY ANOTHER ONE FOR YOUR MEAL.
I USED TO HAVE A CAT, BUT IT DISAPPEARED ONE DAY, ONLY TO HAVE ITS FUR RETURNED TO ME...
APPARENTLY, MY NEIGHBOR ATE MY CAT.
SERIOUSLY?!
COME TO THINK OF IT, WE USED TO DO THE SAME THING TO COWS.
IZUMI-SAN! WILL YOU TELL US WHAT'S RECOMMENDED AT THIS RESTAURANT?!
I guess we shouldn't feel sorry for the cats and dogs after all.
THEY EVEN MAKE A DISTINCTION BETWEEN OLD CAT AND YOUNG CAT! HOW SOPHISTICATED! CHINA IMPRESSED ME, INDEED.
...
OLD CAT

Hainan Island -- The End

✦LOVE LETTER FROM CHINA✦

HELLO, MY READERS. I AM IZUMI.
FOR THE 30TH ANNIVERSARY OF *BESSATSU SHÔJO COMICS*, I HAVE RECEIVED THIS HONORABLE SPACE, SO HERE IS MY GREETING TO YOU...
I'M IN CHINA RIGHT NOW.
THIS IS MY FOURTH TIME HERE AND I STILL OFTEN FIND MYSELF ASTOUNDED.
I'm visiting my father.
Even though a stranger was already using one spot, an old woman didn't hesitate to join her.
FOR EXAMPLE, IN THE TOILET AT THE SHANGHAI TRAIN STATION
...
...
I WAS ASTOUNDED.
Without raising an eyebrow, the younger lady just finished up. Because there was no door, I could see the entire time.
THEN THERE WAS THE CHOCOLATE I BOUGHT AT THE SUPERMARKET...
CHOCOLATES WITH LIQUEUR INSIDE FOR 8 YUAN PER BOX? THAT'S CHEAP!!
Favorite food
1 yuan = ¥14 = $0.12
Yay Yay
Yay
CHOMP
DAMMIT!! THEY GOT ME!!
A bottle-shaped, plain chocolate. Nothing inside.
DESPITE IT ALL, I STILL LOVE THIS COUNTRY.
WHAT NOW? I BOUGHT 10 BOXES!!

LOVE LETTER FROM CHINA -- THE END

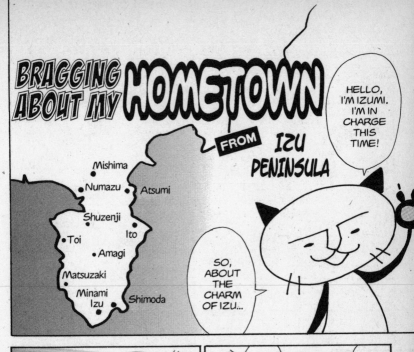

BRAGGING ABOUT MY HOMETOWN
FROM IZU PENINSULA
HELLO, I'M IZUMI. I'M IN CHARGE THIS TIME!
Mishima
Numazu
Atsumi
Shuzenji
Ito
Toi
Amagi
Matsuzaki
Minami Izu
Shimoda
SO, ABOUT THE CHARM OF IZU...
DO YOU EAT SEA-FOOD EVERY DAY?
DOES YOUR FAMILY RUN A HOT SPRING RESORT?
When I was in college, everyone asked the same questions.
Eep!
FLAIL
FLAIL
WRONG! PEOPLE THINK LIFE IS LIKE A TRAVEL GUIDE!!
ZOOM
YOU WANT TO HEAR THE REAL STORY?
WELL, LET ME TELL YOU ABOUT LIFE IN IZU FOR REAL!

FIRST OF ALL, IZU AND THE OCEAN ARE INSEPARABLE.
WHOOOOSH
IT HAS THE MOST TRANSPARENT WATER IN THE KANTO REGION.
I CAN SEE THE TIP OF MY FIN THROUGH THE WAVES.
Shimoda's especially beautiful.
COMPARED WITH HOME, THE WATER AT SHONAN BEACH LOOKED LIKE MISO SOUP TO ME WHEN I FIRST SAW IT.
BECAUSE OF ITS AWESOME BEAUTY, A CERTAIN AREA HAS BECOME FAMOUS FOR SUICIDES--
--STOP! STOP!!
A friend who used to work for a travel agency
But I heard about it when I used to work at the hotel!
Don't write that!
SHALL I CHANGE THE SUBJECT TO SEAFOOD THEN?
YES. TOURISTS LIKE TO HEAR ABOUT FOOD.
HA HA ...
SHOPS CLOSE TO THE SEAPORT SELL FISH THAT IS TRULY FRESH OUT OF THE OCEAN. I HIGHLY RECOMMEND IT!
WOW, STILL LIVELY!
SMALL SHRIMP ¥300
FLOP FLOP

BUT EVEN IN IZU, THERE ARE SOME SHOPS...
LIFE-LESS
...THAT SELL YESTER-DAY'S CATCH, SO PLEASE BE CAREFUL!
BUT REALLY, MOST OF THE EXO-TIC FISH FROM FISH-MONGERS ARE YUMMY!
I like raw octopus in salty spices.
MUNCH
Squid's good, too.
MUNCH
MUNCH
MUNCH
GROWING UP IN THIS AREA, WE ALWAYS WENT TO THE BEACH FOR OUR SCHOOL FIELD TRIPS.
YEAH. AND WE GOT TO COOK MISO SOUP-- BUT WE HAD TO GET OUR FRESH INGREDIENTS FROM THE SEA.
IT WAS LIKE WE WERE REGRESS-ING BACK TO CAVE-MEN!
...
...
Friends REMINISCING
It wasn't like I *set out* to catch the **octopus**, but everyone got mad at me anyway.
* http://69.93.124.90/truestories/hihokan
AFTER VISITING THE OCEAN, YOU MAY WANT TO CHECK OUT THE HOT SPRINGS OFFERED BY THE VARIOUS HOTELS!
You can take a bath even if you're not staying at that hotel so long as you pay for it.
THE FEES ARE PRETTY REASONABLE AND THEY COME WITH DISCOUNT COUPONS FOR THE HOUSE OF HIDDEN TREASURES (?).
IS THE HOUSE OF HIDDEN TREA-SURES A MUSEUM?
I was working at a hotel.
IT'S A MUSEUM... FOR GROWN-UPS.*
HEH HEH

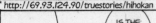

THE IZU PENINSULA IS A LAND OF MOUNTAINS AND OCEAN, AND THERE ARE SCARCELY ANY FLAT AREAS. MUSEUMS AND GALLERIES ARE MOSTLY SMALL.
Entrance fees are usually about ¥300.
THE RELICS ARE ALSO SMALL.
WHO CARES?
YORITOMO MINAMOTO SAT ON THIS STONE
Minamoto was a warrior who lived in the 1100s and founded the shogunate.
BUT ANY-HOW, THIS IS A NICE PLACE. WE HANG OUT HERE ALL THE TIME.
Even though it's a small town.
IF YOU LOOK, YOU CAN FIND CHEAP LODGING, TOO.
HEY, I FOUND SOME RELIGIOUS PAMPHLETS UNDER THE DOOR.
ULP!
It turned out this "motel" was inexpensive because it was actually a religious facility...
(There are a lot of new religious groups in Izu.)
The residents of the facility were parked outside our door, chanting from their booklets.
207
IF YOU THINK IT'S JUST A HIP RESORT AREA, YOU'RE IN FOR A TREAT. IZU IS FULL OF SUR-PRISES.
THE LOCALS WHO LOOK FORWARD TO YOUR VISIT GUARAN-TEE THAT YOU'LL FIND IT WELL WORTH-WHILE.

Bragging About My Hometown -- The End

kaneyoshi izumi

MESSAGE FROM THE AUTHOR

I'd be so happy if I could sunbathe all day long without a care in the world…

ABOUT THE AUTHOR

Kaneyoshi Izumi's birthday is April 1st and her blood type is probably type A (but she hasn't actually had it checked yet). Her debut story "Tenshi" ("Angel") appeared in the September 1995 issue of Bessatsu Shôjo Comics and won the 36th Shogakukan Shinjin ("newbie") Comics Award. Her hobbies include riding motorcycles, playing the piano, and feeding stray cats, and she continues to work as an artist for Bessatsu Shôjo Comics.

HAPPY HUSTLE HIGH™
TOMBOY, INTERRUPTED!
Hanabi Oozora's always acted like a boy, but she's never actually wanted to date one. That is until her all-girls' school gets mixed with an all-boys' school and she meets Yasuaki Garaku!
Unfortunately, he doesn't know (or care) that she's alive. What's a rough-neck girl to do?
ONLY $9.99!
HAPPY HUSTLE HIGH
Happy Hustle High 1
story and art by Rie Takada
store.viz.com
Straight from Japan's top ten sales chart *—start your graphic novel collection today!
VIZ
www.viz.com
* Regularly appeared in Japan's Book Nippan Top Ten sales chart for 2003-2004.
© 2004 Rie Takada/Shogakukan, Inc.

High School Just Got Anime-ted!
The popular shôjo series now available on DVD!
Just as Tsukushi thinks she can attend school unnoticed, the entire school starts bullying her. But when she finds herself in a love triangle with the two most popular boys, that's when the real trouble begins!
Become part of the HANA YORI DANGO crowd – start your DVD collection today!
BOYS over FLOWERS
Hana Yori Dango
Declaration of War!
only $24.98 a volume
DVD VIDEO
TOEI ANIMATION
Since 1956
shôjo
VIZ
www.viz.com
©2004 Yoko Kamio/Shueisha, Toei Animation.

COMPLETE OUR SURVEY AND LET US KNOW WHAT YOU THINK!

☐ Please do NOT send me information about VIZ products, news and events, special offers, or other information.

☐ Please do NOT send me information from VIZ's trusted business partners.

Name: _____

Address: _____

City: _____ **State:** _____ **Zip:** _____

E-mail: _____

☐ Male ☐ Female **Date of Birth (mm/dd/yyyy):** ___ / ___ / ___ (Under 13? Parental consent required)

What race/ethnicity do you consider yourself? (please check one)

☐ Asian/Pacific Islander ☐ Black/African American ☐ Hispanic/Latino

☐ Native American/Alaskan Native ☐ White/Caucasian ☐ Other: _____

What VIZ product did you purchase? (check all that apply and indicate title purchased)

☐ DVD/VHS _____

☐ Graphic Novel _____

☐ Magazines _____

☐ Merchandise _____

Reason for purchase: (check all that apply)

☐ Special offer ☐ Favorite title ☐ Gift

☐ Recommendation ☐ Other _____

Where did you make your purchase? (please check one)

☐ Comic store ☐ Bookstore ☐ Mass/Grocery Store

☐ Newsstand ☐ Video/Video Game Store ☐ Other: _____

☐ Online (site: _____)

What other VIZ properties have you purchased/own? _____

_____

How many anime and/or manga titles have you purchased in the last year? How many were VIZ titles? **(please check one from each column)**

ANIME	MANGA	VIZ
☐ None	☐ None	☐ None
☐ 1-4	☐ 1-4	☐ 1-4
☐ 5-10	☐ 5-10	☐ 5-10
☐ 11+	☐ 11+	☐ 11+

I find the pricing of VIZ products to be: **(please check one)**

☐ Cheap ☐ Reasonable ☐ Expensive

What genre of manga and anime would you like to see from VIZ? **(please check two)**

☐ Adventure ☐ Comic Strip ☐ Science Fiction ☐ Fighting

☐ Horror ☐ Romance ☐ Fantasy ☐ Sports

What do you think of VIZ's new look?

☐ Love It ☐ It's OK ☐ Hate It ☐ Didn't Notice ☐ No Opinion

Which do you prefer? **(please check one)**

☐ Reading right-to-left

☐ Reading left-to-right

Which do you prefer? **(please check one)**

☐ Sound effects in English

☐ Sound effects in Japanese with English captions

☐ Sound effects in Japanese only with a glossary at the back

THANK YOU! Please send the completed form to:

VIZ Survey
42 Catharine St.
Poughkeepsie, NY 12601

All information provided will be used for internal purposes only. We promise not to sell or otherwise divulge your information.